POLAR ANIMALS

SEALS
ARE AWESOME

by Jaclyn Jaycox

Consultant: Greg Breed
Associate Professor of Ecology
Institute of Arctic Biology
University of Alaska, Fairbanks

PEBBLE
a capstone imprint

A+ Books are published by Pebble,
1710 Roe Crest Drive, North Mankato, Minnesota 56003
www.mycapstone.com

Library of Congress Cataloging-in-Publication Data
Names: Jaycox, Jaclyn, 1983–author.
Title: Seals Are Awesome / by Jaclyn Jaycox.
Description: North Mankato, Minnesota: an imprint of Pebble, [2020] |
    Series: A+. Polar Animals | Audience: Age 4–8. | Audience: K to Grade 3. |
    Includes bibliographical references and index.
Identifiers: LCCN 2018056756| ISBN 9781977108203 (hardcover) | ISBN
    9781977110008 (paperback) | ISBN 9781977108296 (ebook pdf)
Subjects: LCSH: Seals (Animals)—Juvenile literature. | Animals—Polar
    regions—Juvenile literature.
Classification: LCC QL737.P64 J39 2020 | DDC 599.79)—dc23
LC record available at https://lccn.loc.gov/2018056756

Editorial Credits
Nikki Potts, editor; Kayla Rossow, designer; Morgan Walters, media researcher;
Laura Manthe, production specialist

Photo Credits
Alamy: Hemis, 8, Nature Picture Library, 17, 19; Newscom: Tui De Roy/ Minden Pictures, 13; Shutterstock: BMJ, 28, Darren Begley, 9, Dolores Harvey, 4, 10, Enrique Aguirre, 7, 29, evenfh, 14, FloridaStock, 23, Incredible Arctic, spread 24-25, Mara008, design element (blue), Marcos Amend, 18, Mariusz Potocki, 5, NicoElNino, 6, Oliay, design element (ice window), Ondrej Prosicky, Cover, 11, photosoft, design element (ice), polarman, 20, bottom right 22, Tarpan, bottom right 26, Vladimir Melnik, 21, top 22, left 26, vladsilver, 12, spread 14-15, Yongyut Kumsri, spread 26-27

All internet sites appearing in back matter were available and accurate when this book was sent to press.

Note to Parents, Teachers, and Librarians

This Polar Animals book uses full-color photographs and a nonfiction format to introduce the concept of seals. *Seals Are Awesome* is designed to be read aloud to a pre-reader or to be read independently by an early reader. Photographs help listeners and early readers understand the text and concepts discussed. The book encourages further learning by including the following sections: Table of Contents, Glossary, Read More, Internet Sites, Critical Thinking Questions, and Index. Early readers may need assistance using these features.

Printed in China.
1671

TABLE OF CONTENTS

Life in the Ocean

Splash! Seals spend most of their lives in the water. Most seals can hold their breath for more than 30 minutes. Seals can even sleep underwater. They rise to the surface to breathe without waking up. *Zzz.*

Ice Seals

Many types of seals are found on polar sea ice. Four types of seals live in the Antarctic. They are the Weddell, Ross, leopard, and crabeater seals.

Six types of seals live
in the Arctic. Ribbon,
hooded, ringed, harp,
bearded, and spotted
seals can be found there.

Ringed seals are the smallest polar ice seals. They weigh less than 150 pounds (68 kilograms).

Leopard seals are the largest. They can weigh up to 1,300 pounds (590 kg). That is as heavy as a polar bear!

Seals have large bodies.
They have front and back
flippers to help them swim.
Seals also have claws.
Claws help them crawl out
of the water onto land.

Seals can't move well on land. They use their front flippers and claws to drag their bodies around.

Seals have a thick layer of blubber. It keeps them warm. Even in the freezing weather, they can get too hot. They jump into the icy water to cool off.

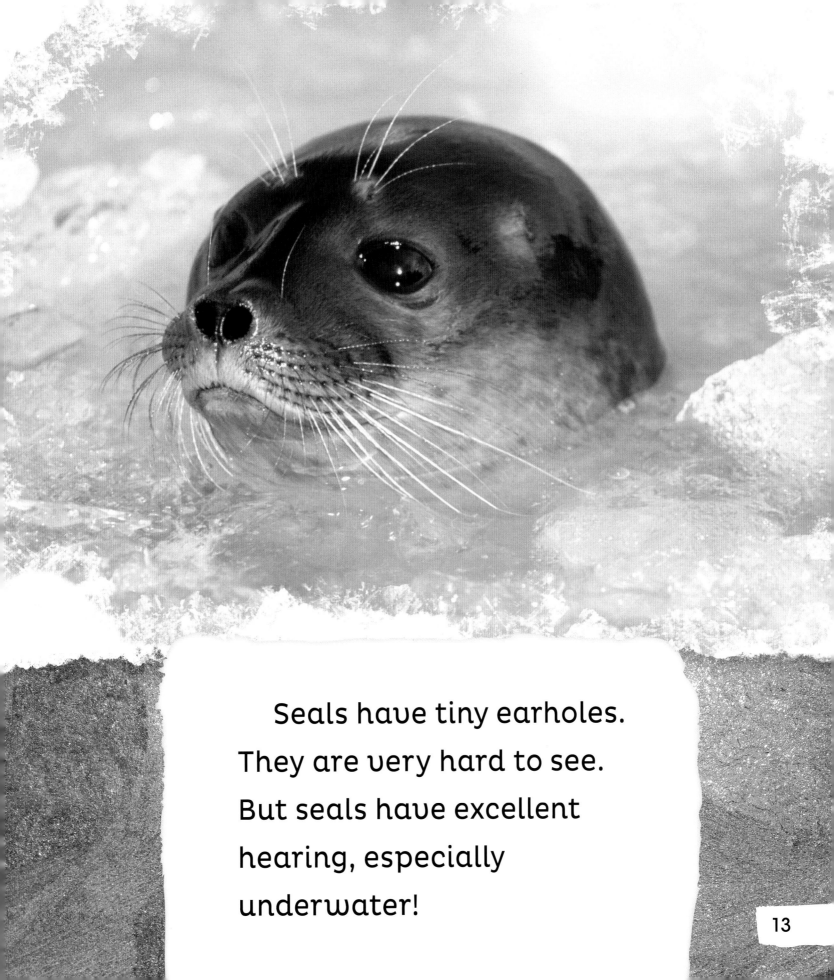

Seals have tiny earholes.
They are very hard to see.
But seals have excellent
hearing, especially
underwater!

Polar ice seals can have brown, cream, or gray skin. Their skin can be solid or spotted. The leopard seal gets its name from its spots. The ringed seal has circle patterns on its back. Most seals also have a layer of waterproof fur.

Finding Food

Seals dive deep into the ocean to find food. Some can dive up to 2,000 feet (600 meters). Seals use their whiskers to find prey in the dark water. Whiskers help them feel movement in the water. Seals can swim up to 23 miles per hour (37 kilometers per hour) to catch food.

Seals have strong jaws
and sharp teeth. Most seals
eat fish, squid, and krill.

Leopard seals will also
eat seal pups and penguins.
Seals catch most of their
food underwater.

Family Life

Seals mate and give birth on the ice. Females have one baby at a time. A baby seal is called a pup.

The mother calls to her
pup after it's born. The pup
learns her sound. If the
pup gets lost, it will be
able to find its mother
from her call.

Mothers stay on the ice
with their pup. Pups drink
milk from their mothers.
Pups grow quickly.

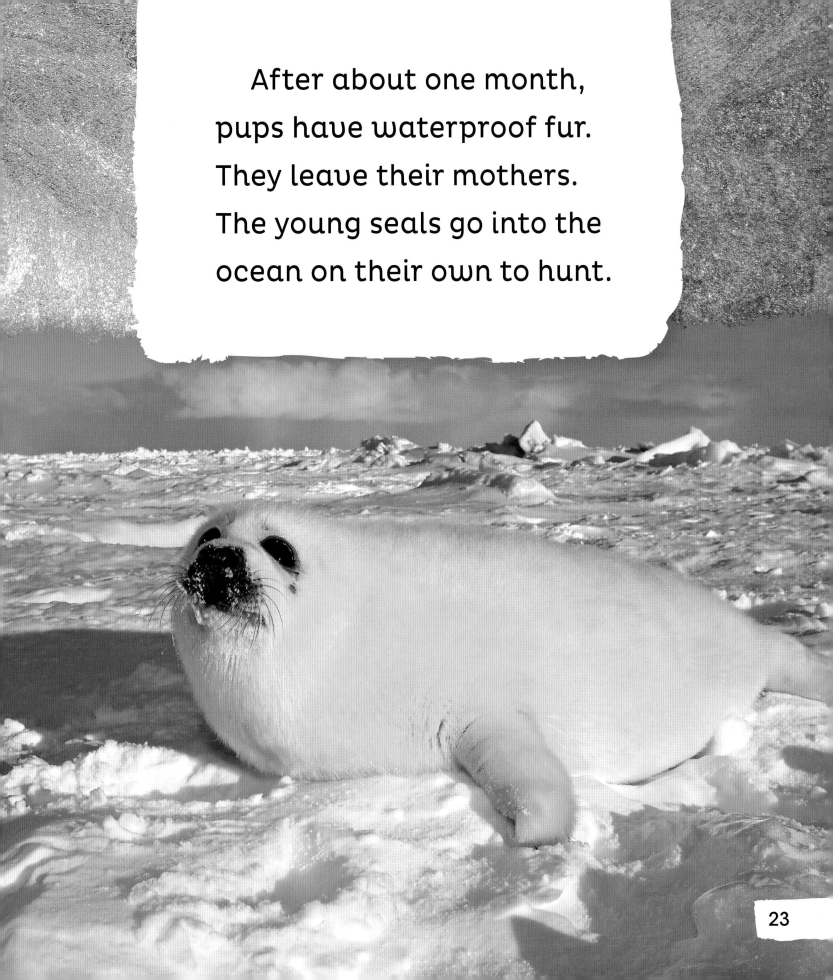

After about one month,
pups have waterproof fur.
They leave their mothers.
The young seals go into the
ocean on their own to hunt.

Staying Safe

Seals can live more than 30 years. But the changing climate is a danger to seals. They need the ice to mate and have young. As temperatures rise, polar ice melts. Seals' habitat is getting smaller. This could mean fewer pups will be born.

Seals need lots of food to keep their blubber. Krill are being caught by fishermen. Seals may not have enough to eat to stay warm.

krill

Seals have few
predators. But hungry
killer whales or polar bears
may try to snatch them.

Seals live in the coldest places on Earth. Blubber helps keep them warm in the freezing water.

There are 33 different types of seals. Only 10 of these are tough enough for the polar regions.

GLOSSARY

Antarctic (ANT-ark-tik)—having to do with the South Pole or the region around it

Arctic (ARK-tik)—the area near the North Pole; the Arctic is cold and covered with ice

blubber (BLUH-buhr)—a thick layer of fat under the skin of some animals; blubber keeps animals warm

climate (KLY-muht)—the average weather of a place throughout the year

female (FEE-male)—an animal that can give birth to young animals or lay eggs

flipper (FLIP-ur)—one of the broad, flat limbs of an ocean or freshwater animal

habitat (HAB-uh-tat)—the natural place and conditions in which a plant or animal lives

krill (KRIL)—a small shrimplike animal

mate (MATE)—to join together to produce young

polar (POH-lur)—having to do with the icy regions around the North or South Pole

predator (PRED-uh-tur)—an animal that hunts other animals for food

prey (PRAY)—an animal hunted by another animal for food

READ MORE

Clay, Kathryn. *Seals: A 4D Book*. Mammals in the Wild. North Mankato, MN: Capstone Press, 2019.

King, Aven. *Harp Seals*. Ocean Friends. New York: PowerKids Press, 2016.

Statts, Leo. *Seals*. Zoom in on Polar Animals. Minneapolis: Abdo Zoom, 2017.

INTERNET SITES

DK Find Out, Seals
https://www.dkfindout.com/us/animals-and-nature/seals-sea-lions-and-walruses/seals/

National Geographic Kids, Harp Seal Profile
https://kids.nationalgeographic.com/animals/harp-seal/#harp-seal-closeup.jpg

CRITICAL THINKING QUESTIONS

1. What types of seals can be found in the Antarctic?

2. What types of seals can be found in the Arctic?

3. How do seals stay warm in the icy water?

4. What do seals eat?

INDEX